Annie's

Quick & Easy Quilts

LEISURE ARTS, INC. • Maumelle, Arkansas

Quick & Easy Quilts is a collection of fun, fast and fabulous quilts perfect for a rainy day, a free weekend or anytime you want to quilt and feel that sense of accomplishment for actually finishing a project. You'll find 12 projects to select from, and all you have to do is add the time and the fabric. There's everything from traditional to contemporary quilt styles of all skill levels, and many are scrap friendly. This book offers everything you could possibly want in a quick and easy quilt project.

HAPPY QUILTING.

ANNIE'S STAFF

EDITOR **Carolyn S. Vagts**
CREATIVE DIRECTOR **Brad Snow**
PUBLISHING SERVICES DIRECTOR **Brenda Gallmeyer**
MANAGING EDITOR **Barb Sprunger**
TECHNICAL EDITOR **Angie Buckles**
COPY MANAGER **Corene Painter**
SENIOR COPY EDITOR **Emily Carter**
TECHNICAL ARTIST **Amanda Joseph**
SENIOR PRODUCTION ARTIST **Nicole Gage**
PRODUCTION ASSISTANTS **Laurie Lehman, Marj Morgan, Judy Neuenschwander**
PHOTOGRAPHY SUPERVISOR **Tammy Christian**
PHOTOGRAPHY **Matthew Owen**
PHOTO STYLISTS **Tammy Liechty, Tammy Steiner**

CHIEF EXECUTIVE OFFICER **David McKee**
EXECUTIVE VICE PRESIDENT **Michele Fortune**

LEISURE ARTS STAFF
Editorial Staff

CREATIVE ART DIRECTOR **Katherine Laughlin**
PUBLICATIONS DIRECTOR **Leah Lampirez**
SPECIAL PROJECTS DIRECTOR **Susan Frantz Wiles**
PREPRESS TECHNICIAN **Stephanie Johnson**

Business Staff

PRESIDENT AND CHIEF EXECUTIVE OFFICER **Fred F. Pruss**
SENIOR VICE PRESIDENT OF OPERATIONS **Jim Dittrich**
VICE PRESIDENT OF RETAIL SALES **Martha Adams**
CHIEF FINANCIAL OFFICER **Tiffany P. Childers**
CONTROLLER **Teresa Eby**
INFORMATION TECHNOLOGY DIRECTOR **Brian Roden**
DIRECTOR OF E-COMMERCE **Mark Hawkins**
MANAGER OF E-COMMERCE **Robert Young**

ISBN-13/EAN: 978-1-4647-3335-2
UPC: 0-28906-06442-1

PROJECTS

4

Stunning Stars
A fat quarter friendly project.

8

Optica
A twist on a classic Nine-Patch.

12

Quick Step
Add just a touch of appliqué.

16

Summer Dreams Rail Fence
Black-and-white with a touch of bright.

20

Corporal's Stripes
Twist and turn a single block.

24

Walk Around the Block
Make it in a weekend.

27

Woven Indigo
Traditional colors, modern look.

30

Nine-Patch Twirl
A simple Nine-Patch variation.

33

Chocolate Covered Cherries
A sweet treat with one
simple block.

36

Go Team!
Show your favorite team's colors.

39

Seven-Patch
This quilt has a single block
pattern with seven pieces.

43

Summer Shores
Showcase a favorite fabric
collection.

Quilting Basics, **46**

Stunning Stars

This variation of a Friendship Star block, a six-pack of fat quarters and a background fabric make the perfect lap quilt or, with the right fabrics, a fun baby quilt.

Design by Nancy Scott

Skill Level
Confident Beginner

Finished Size
Quilt Size: 39" x 48"
Block Size: 9" x 9" finished
Number of Blocks: 12

CUTTING

From dark purple tonal:
• Cut 3 (3⅞" x 21") strips.
  Subcut into 12 (3⅞") D squares.

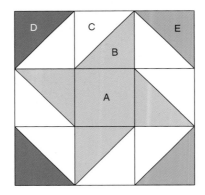

Side Star
9" x 9" Finished Block
Make 6

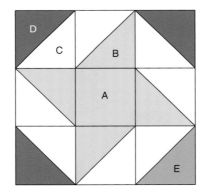

Corner Star
9" x 9" Finished Block
Make 4

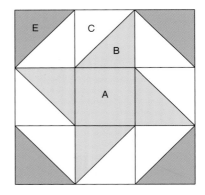

Friendship Star
9" x 9" Finished Block
Make 2

From aqua print:
- Cut 3 (3⅞" x 21") strips.
  Subcut into 12 (3⅞") E squares.

From 1 pastel tonal:
- Cut 9 (1½" x 21") H/I strips.

From 3 remaining pastel tonals:
- Cut 1 (3½" x 21") strip.
  Subcut into 4 (3½") A squares each fabric to total 12.
- Cut 2 (3⅞" x 21") strips.
  Subcut into 8 (3⅞") B squares each fabric to total 24.

From white solid:
- Cut 1 piece 45" by fabric width.
  Subcut along length into 4 (2½" x 45") strips. Trim strips to make 2 (2½" x 36½") F strips and 2 (2½" x 31½") G strips.
  From the remaining 45" piece, cut 4 (3½" x 45") J/K strips along length. Trim strips to make 2 (3½" x 42½") J strips and 2 (3½" x 39½") K strips.
  From the remaining 45" piece, cut 5 (2¼" x 45") binding strips along length.
  Subcut the remainder of the 45" piece into 11 (3⅞") C squares.
- Cut 4 (3⅞" by fabric width) strips from the remaining yardage.
  Subcut into an additional 37 (3⅞") C squares (total 48 C squares).

COMPLETING THE BLOCKS

1. Draw a diagonal line from corner to corner on the wrong side of each C square.
2. Referring to Figure 1, place a C square right sides together with a B square and stitch ¼" on each side of the marked line; cut apart on the marked line and press the units open with seams away from C to complete two B-C units. Repeat with all B squares to complete a total of 48 B-C units.

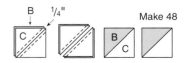

Figure 1

3. Repeat step 2 with C and D to make 24 C-D units and with C and E to make 24 C-E units referring to Figure 2.

Make 24 each

Figure 2

4. Select one A square, four B-C units to match A and four C-E units to make a Friendship Star block.
5. Sew a B-C unit to opposite sides of A to make the center row referring to Figure 3; press seams toward A.

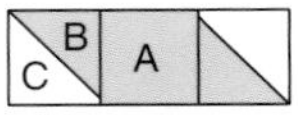

Figure 3 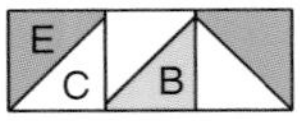   **Figure 4**

6. Sew a C-E unit to opposite sides of a B-C unit to make the top row as shown in Figure 4; press seams toward C-E. Repeat to make the bottom row.
7. Join the rows, referring to Figure 5, to complete one block; press.

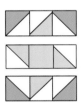

Figure 5

8. Repeat steps 4–7 to complete a second block.
9. Select one A square, four B-C units to match A, one C-E unit and three C-D units to complete one Corner Star block.
10. Refer to steps 5–7 and Figure 6 to complete one block; press. Repeat to make a total of four Corner Star blocks.

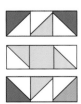

Figure 6

11. Select one A square, four B-C units to match A and two each C-E units and C-D units to complete one Side Star block.

12. Refer to steps 5–7 and Figure 7 to complete one block; press. Repeat to make a total of six Side Star blocks.

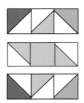

Figure 7

COMPLETING THE QUILT

1. Arrange and join the Friendship Star, Corner Star and Side Star blocks in four rows of three blocks each referring to the Assembly Diagram; press.

2. Join the rows to complete the pieced center; press.

3. Sew F strips to opposite long sides and G strips to the top and bottom of the pieced center; press seams toward strips.

4. Join the H/I strips on the short ends with diagonal seams as shown in Figure 8; press seams open. Subcut strip into two 1½" x 40½" H strips and two 1½" x 33½" I strips.

Figure 8

5. Sew H strips to opposite long sides and I strips to the top and bottom of the pieced center; press seam toward strips.

6. Sew J strips to opposite long sides and K strips to the top and bottom of the pieced center to complete the quilt top; press seams toward strips.

7. Create a quilt sandwich referring to Quilting Basics on page 46.

8. Quilt as desired.

9. Bind referring to Quilting Basics on page 46 to finish. ●

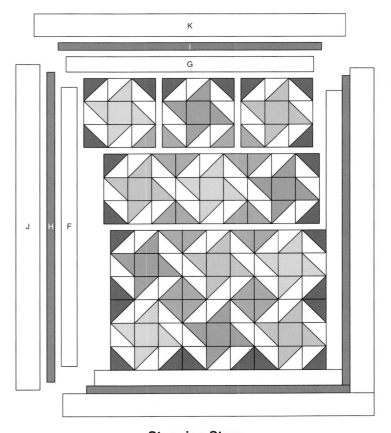

Stunning Stars
Assembly Diagram 39" x 48"

Optica

A contemporary quilt made with a classic and timeless Nine-Patch block—now that's a novel idea!

Design by Tricia Lynn Maloney

Skill Level
Beginner

Finished Size
Quilt Size: 60" x 60"
Block Size: 12" x 12" finished
Number of Blocks: 16

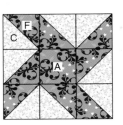

Optica 1
12" x 12" Finished Block
Make 4

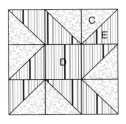

Optica 2
12" x 12" Finished Block
Make 8

MATERIALS

- ⅞ yard coordinating mini-print
- 1⅓ yards coordinating light floral
- 1⅓ yards coordinating stripe
- 1⅜ yards dark floral
- Backing to size
- Batting to size
- Thread
- Basic sewing tools and supplies

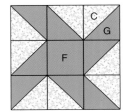

Optica 3
12" x 12" Finished Block
Make 4

CUTTING

From mini-print:
- Cut 2 (4⅞" by fabric width) strips.
  Subcut strips into 16 (4⅞") G squares.
- Cut 1 (4½" by fabric width) strip.
  Subcut strips into 4 (4½") F squares.
- Cut 5 (2½" by fabric width) K strips.

From light floral:
- Cut 8 (4⅞" by fabric width) strips.
  Subcut strips into 64 (4⅞") C squares.
- Cut 1 (4½" by fabric width) strip.
  Subcut strip into 4 (4½") H squares.

From stripe:
- Cut 4 (4⅞" by fabric width) strips.
  Subcut strips into 32 (4⅞") E squares.
- Cut 1 (4½" by fabric width) strip.
  Subcut strip into 8 (4½") D squares.
- Cut 7 (2¼" by fabric width) binding strips.

From dark floral:
- Cut 2 (4⅞" by fabric width) strips.
  Subcut strips into 16 (4⅞") B squares.
- Cut 6 (4½" by fabric width) strips.
  Subcut one strip into 4 (4½") A squares. Use five strips for L.
- Cut 2 (2½" by fabric width) strips.
  Subcut strips into 4 (2½" by 4½") I rectangles and 4 (2½" by 6½") J rectangles.

COMPLETING THE BLOCKS

1. Draw a diagonal on the wrong side of each C square.
2. Layer a C square right sides together with a B square and stitch a ¼" seam on both sides of the diagonal line as shown in Figure 1.

Figure 1

3. Cut on the diagonal line to make two B-C squares, again referring to Figure 1. Press seams toward B.
4. Repeat steps 2 and 3 with all B, C, E and G squares to make 32 B-C squares, 64 C-E squares and 32 C-G squares referring to Figure 2. Label and set aside C-E and C-G squares.

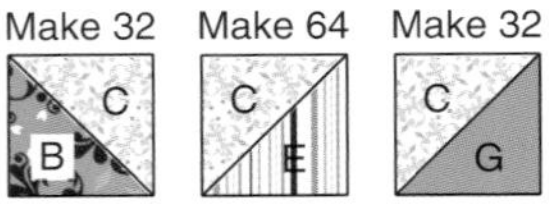

Make 32   Make 64   Make 32

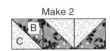

Make 2

Figure 2   **Figure 3**

5. Stitch two B-C squares together matching the B sides. Stitch another B-C square, matching the C sides as shown in Figure 3 to make top row. Repeat to make bottom row.

Figure 4

6. Stitch an A square between two B-C squares, matching B sides to opposite A sides to make center row as shown in Figure 4.

7. Stitch center row between top and bottom rows as shown in Figure 5, matching B edges of the B-C rows to A to make an Optica 1 block.

Figure 5

8. Repeat steps 5–7 to make four Optica 1 blocks.
9. Repeat steps 5–7 with D and C-E squares to make eight Optica 2 blocks referring to the block drawing.
10. Repeat steps 5–7 with F and C-G squares to make four Optica 3 blocks referring to the block drawing.

COMPLETING THE QUILT

1. Arrange and join one each Optica 1 and Optica 3 block and two Optica 2 blocks to make an X row referring to Figure 6. Repeat to make two X rows.

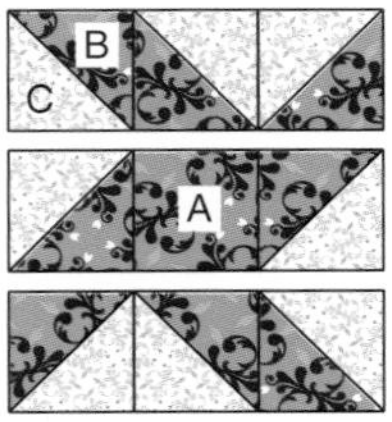

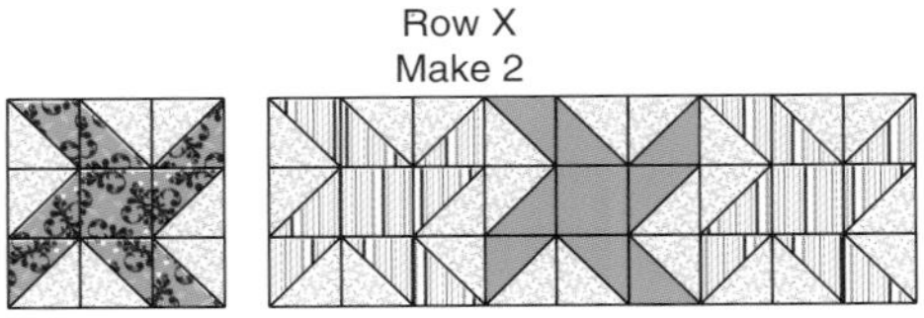

Row X
Make 2

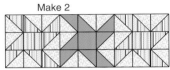

Figure 6

2. Arrange and join one each Optica 1 and Optica 3 block and two Optica 2 blocks to make a Y row referring to Figure 7. Repeat to make two Y rows.

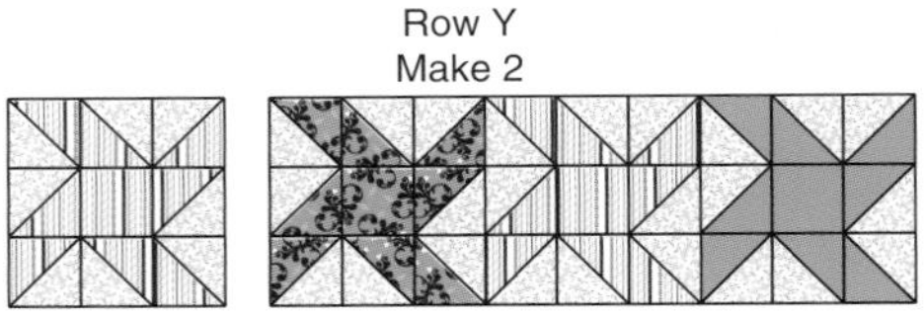

Row Y
Make 2

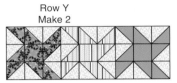

Figure 7

3. Arrange rows as shown in Figure 8. ***Note:** Reverse third and fourth rows as indicated.*

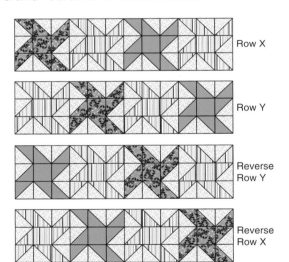

Row X

Row Y

Reverse Row Y

Reverse Row X

Figure 8

4. Stitch rows together as arranged, matching seams, to complete the pieced center. Press seams in one direction.

5. Stitch an I rectangle to the bottom of H as shown in Figure 9. Press seam toward I.

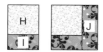

Figure 9

6. Sew a J rectangle to one side of the H-I unit, again referring to Figure 9. Press seam toward J.
7. Repeat steps 5 and 6 to make four H-I-J corner units.
8. Join the L strips together on short ends to make one long strip; press seams open. Subcut strip into four 4½" x 48½" L border strips.
9. Join the K strips together on short ends to make one long strip; press seams open. Subcut strip into four 2½" x 48½" K border strips.

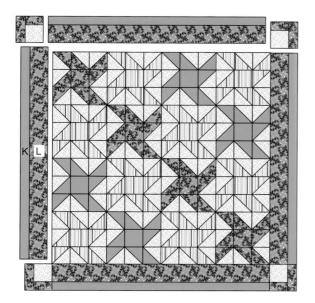

Optica
Assembly Diagram 60" x 60"

10. Stitch an L border strip to a K border strip along length to make an L-K border strip; press seam toward L. Repeat to make four L-K border strips.
11. Stitch an L-K border strip to opposite sides of the pieced center referring to Figure 10.

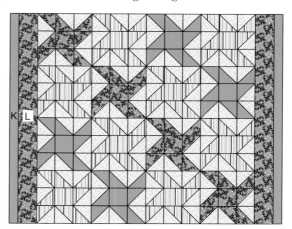

Figure 10

12. Stitch an H-I-J corner unit to both ends of the remaining L-K border strips to make top and bottom borders referring to Figure 11.

Make 2

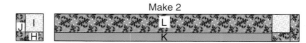

Figure 11

13. Stitch the top and bottom borders to the pieced center referring to the Assembly Diagram.
14. Create a quilt sandwich referring to Quilting Basics on page 46.
15. Quilt as desired.
16. Bind referring to Quilting Basics on page 46 to finish. ●

Quick Step

A traditionally pieced block pattern, a white solid background and a touch of fusible appliqué is all you need to create this lovely quilt.

Design by Gina Gempesaw

Skill Level
Confident Beginner

Finished Size
Quilt Size: 73" x 91½"
Block Size: 16" x 16" finished
Number of Blocks: 12

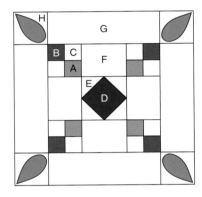

Teardrop
16" x 16" Finished Block
Make 12

MATERIALS

- ½ yard dark green solid
- ⅝ yard light purple solid
- ¾ yard light green solid
- 1⅛ yards dark purple solid
- 5¾ yards white solid
- Backing to size
- Batting to size
- Thread
- Invisible thread (optional)
- 1 yard 18"-wide paper-backed fusible web
- Template material
- Basic sewing tools and supplies

CUTTING

From dark green solid:
- Cut 3 (2" by fabric width) B strips.
- Cut 2 (3" by fabric width) strips.
  Subcut strips into 20 (3") J squares.

From light green solid:
- Cut 3 (2" by fabric width) A strips.
- Cut 7 (2" by fabric width) K/L strips.

From dark purple solid:
- Cut 1 (3⅜" by fabric width) strip.
  Subcut strip into 12 (3⅜") D squares.
- Cut 9 (2¼" by fabric width) binding strips.

From white solid:
- Cut 6 (2" by fabric width) C strips.
- Cut 2 (2⅞" by fabric width) strips.
  Subcut strips into 24 (2⅞") squares. Cut each square in half on 1 diagonal to make 48 E triangles.
- Cut 4 (4½" by fabric width) strips.
  Subcut strips into 48 (3½" x 4½") F rectangles.
- Cut 4 (10½" by fabric width) strips.
  Subcut strips into 48 (3½" by 10½") G strips.
- Cut 16 (3" by fabric width) strips.
  Subcut strips into 31 (3" x 16½") I strips.
- Cut 2 (6½" x 80") M strips and 2 (6½" x 73½") N strips along the length.

- Cut 3 (4" by fabric length) strips from leftover width. Subcut strips into 48 (4") H squares. **Note:** *The H squares will be trimmed after teardrop shapes have been appliquéd to them.*

COMPLETING THE APPLIQUÉ

1. Prepare a template for the teardrop pattern given on page 15. Trace the teardrop shape on the paper side of fusible web 48 times.
2. Fuse the traced teardrops to the wrong side of the light purple solid; cut out on traced lines and remove paper backing.
3. Center diagonally and fuse one teardrop onto an H square. Stitch the teardrop in place using your favorite appliqué method. **Note:** *The sample used invisible thread and a machine blanket stitch for appliqué.*
4. When all teardrops have been appliquéd, trim H to 3½" square, keeping the teardrop centered on the diagonal of the square.

COMPLETING THE TEARDROP BLOCKS

1. Sew a B strip to a C strip along the length to make a B-C strip set; press seam toward B. Repeat to make a total of three B-C strip sets.
2. Subcut the B-C strip sets into 48 (2") B-C units as shown in Figure 1.

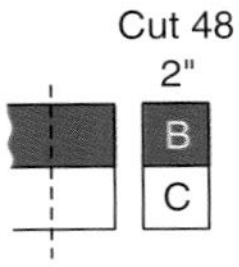

Cut 48
2"

Figure 1

3. Sew an A strip to a C strip along the length to make an A-C strip set; press seams toward A. Repeat to make a total of three A-C strip sets.
4. Subcut the A-C strip sets into 48 (2") A-C units as shown in Figure 2.

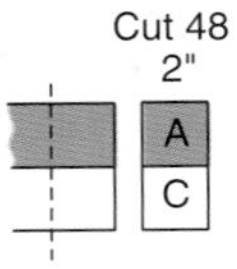

Cut 48
2"

Make 48

Figure 2 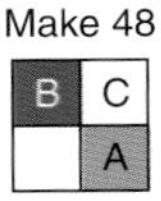   **Figure 3**

5. Select and join one each A-C and B-C unit to complete a Four-Patch unit as shown in Figure 3; press seam to one side. Repeat to make a total of 48 Four-Patch units.

6. Sew an E triangle to each side of a D square to make a D-E unit as shown in Figure 4; press seams toward E. Repeat to make a total of 12 D-E units. **Note:** *The D-E unit should measure 4½" square.*

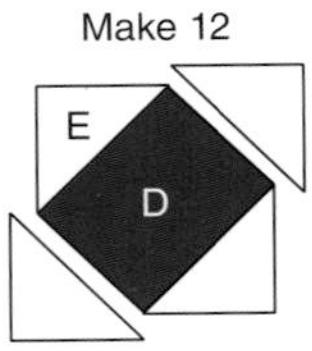

Make 12

Figure 4

7. To complete one Teardrop block, select one D-E unit, four Four-Patch units, four appliquéd H squares and four each F and G pieces.
8. Sew an F rectangle to opposite sides of the D-E unit to complete the center row as shown in Figure 5; press seams toward F.

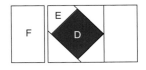   

Make 2

Figure 5   **Figure 6**

9. Sew a Four-Patch unit to opposite sides of an F rectangle to make the top row referring to Figure 6; press seams toward F. Repeat to make the bottom row.
10. Sew the top and bottom rows to the center row to complete the block center referring to Figure 7; press seams away from the center row.

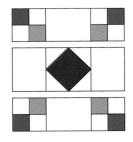   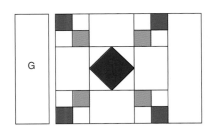

Figure 7   **Figure 8**

11. Sew a G strip to opposite sides of the block center referring to Figure 8; press seams toward G.

12. Sew an appliquéd H square to each end of two G strips referring to Figure 9; press seams toward G.

Figure 9

13. Sew the G-H units to opposite sides of the block center to complete one Teardrop block referring to Figure 10; press seams toward the G-H units.

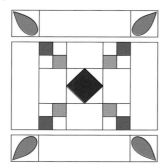

Figure 10

14. Repeat steps 7–13 to complete a total of 12 Teardrop blocks.

COMPLETING THE QUILT

1. Join three Teardrop blocks with four I strips to make a block row as shown in Figure 11; press seams toward I. Repeat to make a total of four block rows.

Make 4

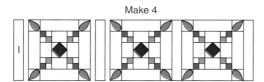

Figure 11

2. Join three I strips with four J squares to make a sashing row referring to Figure 12; press seams toward I. Repeat to make a total of five sashing rows.

Make 5

Figure 12

3. Join the block rows with the sashing rows to complete the pieced center referring to the Placement Diagram for positioning; press seams toward sashing strips.

4. Join the K/L strips on the short ends to make a long strip; press seams open. Subcut strip into two 2" x 77" K strips and two 2" x 61½" L strips.

5. Sew K strips to opposite long sides and L strips to the top and bottom of the pieced center; press seams toward K and L strips.

6. Sew M strips to opposite long sides and N strips to the top and bottom of the pieced center to complete the quilt top; press seams toward the M and N strips.

7. Create a quilt sandwich referring to Quilting Basics on page 46.

8. Quilt as desired.

9. Bind referring to Quilting Basics on page 46 to finish. ●

Quick Step
Teardrop
Cut 48 light purple solid

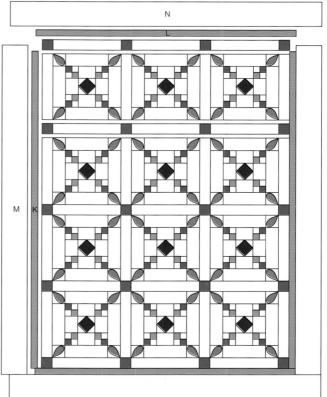

Quick Step
Assembly Diagram 73" x 91½"

Summer Dreams Rail Fence

A child's beach theme vision inspired this colorful kid-friendly quilt.

Design by Bev Getschel

Skill Level
Beginner

Finished Size
Quilt Size: 58" x 78"
Block Size: 10" x 10" finished
Number of Blocks: 24

MATERIALS

- ½ yard each raspberry, blue, orange, yellow & green mottleds
- ⅝ yard black tonal
- 5 yards total white-with-black and black-with-white prints (½ yard cuts of 10 fabrics, 20 fat quarters or scraps)
- Backing to size
- Batting to size
- Thread
- 2½ yards 18"-wide paper-backed fusible web
- Basic sewing tools and supplies

CUTTING

Prepare templates for Flower, Fish, Heart, Sun, Sun Ray, Triangle and Star using patterns provided on page 19 referring to Quilting Basics on page 46. Cut from fabric as indicated on patterns.

From black tonal:
- Cut 7 (2¼" by 42") binding strips.

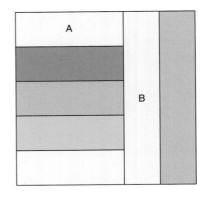

Rail Fence
10" x 10" Finished Block
Make 24

From white-with-black & black-with-white prints:
- Cut 44 (5½" x 7") E rectangles.
- Cut 4 (7") F squares
- Cut 3"-wide C/D strips by fabric piece widths to total 230".
- Cut 120 (2½" x 6½") A rectangles.
- Cut 48 (2½" x 10½") B strips.

COMPLETING THE RAIL FENCE BLOCKS

1. Select five A and two B pieces for one block.
2. Join the five A pieces along length to make an A unit; press seams in one direction.
3. Join two B pieces along length to make a B unit; press seam to one side.
4. Join the A unit with the B unit referring to the block drawing to complete one Rail Fence block; press seams toward B unit.
5. Repeat steps 1–4 to complete 24 Rail Fence blocks.

COMPLETING THE PIECED CENTER

1. Join four Rail Fence blocks to complete a W row referring to Figure 1; press seams in one direction. Repeat to make two W rows. Repeat to make two X, one Y and one Z row, again referring to Figure 1.
2. Join the W, X, Y and Z rows referring to the Placement Diagram to complete the pieced center; press seams in one direction.

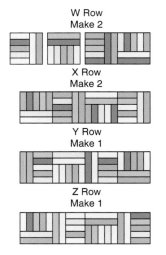

W Row
Make 2

X Row
Make 2

Y Row
Make 1

Z Row
Make 1

Figure 1

COMPLETING THE QUILT

1. Join the C/D strips on short ends to make one long strip; press seams open. Subcut strip into two 60½" C strips and two 45½" D strips.
2. Sew C strips to opposite long sides and D strips to the top and bottom of the pieced center; press seams toward C and D strips.
3. Prepare templates for appliqué shapes using patterns given.
4. Trace appliqué shapes onto the paper side of the fusible web referring to patterns for number to cut; cut out shapes, leaving a margin around each one.
5. Fuse shapes to the wrong side of fabrics as directed for color; cut out shapes on traced lines. Remove paper backing.
6. Fuse shapes to the E rectangles and F squares, arranging the sun rays on E or F before fusing the sun shape in place on top referring to Figure 2 and the Placement Diagram for positioning.

Figure 2

7. Using a narrow zigzag stitch and thread to match appliqué shapes, machine-stitch around each fused shape.
8. Arrange and join 13 appliquéd E rectangles to make a side row referring to the Placement Diagram for positioning; press seams in one direction. Repeat to make two side rows.
9. Sew a side row to opposite long sides of the pieced center; press seams toward C strips.

10. Arrange and join nine appliquéd E rectangles; press seams in one direction. Add an appliquéd F square to each end to complete the top row; press seams away from F. Repeat to make the bottom row.
11. Sew the top and bottom rows to the top and bottom of the pieced center; press seams toward D strips.
12. Arrange triangle shapes on the Rail Fence blocks referring to the Placement Diagram for positioning suggestions; fuse in place.
13. Using a narrow zigzag stitch and thread to match triangle shapes, machine-stitch around each fused triangle to complete the pieced top.
14. Create a quilt sandwich referring to Quilting Basics on page 46.
15. Quilt as desired.
16. Bind referring to Quilting Basics on page 46 to finish. ●

Summer Dreams Rail Fence
Assembly Diagram 58" x 78"

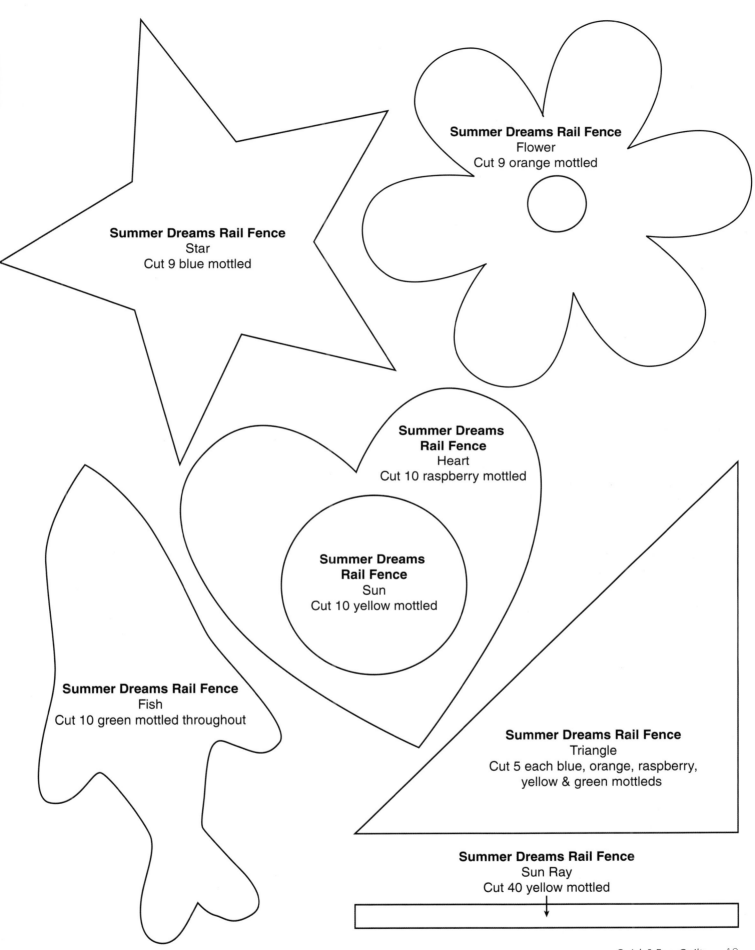

Summer Dreams Rail Fence
Star
Cut 9 blue mottled

Summer Dreams Rail Fence
Flower
Cut 9 orange mottled

**Summer Dreams
Rail Fence**
Heart
Cut 10 raspberry mottled

**Summer Dreams
Rail Fence**
Sun
Cut 10 yellow mottled

Summer Dreams Rail Fence
Fish
Cut 10 green mottled throughout

Summer Dreams Rail Fence
Triangle
Cut 5 each blue, orange, raspberry,
yellow & green mottleds

Summer Dreams Rail Fence
Sun Ray
Cut 40 yellow mottled

Corporal's Stripes

The rank of corporal is reserved for squad leaders in certain branches of the United States Army and Marines. This quilt's light stripes are perfect to use for signatures of squadron members, if desired.

Design by Renelda Peldunas-Harter

Skill Level
Beginner

Finished Size
Quilt Size: 48½" x 63½"
Block Size: 6" x 6⅜" finished
Number of Blocks: 48

MATERIALS

- 1⅓ yards light brown tonal
- 1¼ yards tan tonal
- 1⅝ yards dark brown tonal
- Backing to size
- Batting to size
- Thread
- Basic sewing tools and supplies

CUTTING

From light brown:
- Cut 10 (2½" x 43") C strips.
- Cut 2 (3¾" x 42½") H strips.
- Cut 3 (3¾" x 43") I strips.

From tan:
- Cut 10 (2½" x 43") B strips.
- Cut 2 (2½" x 36½") D strips.
- Cut 3 (2½" x 43") E strips.

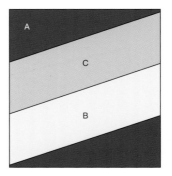

Reversed Stripes
6" x 6⅜" Finished Block
Make 24

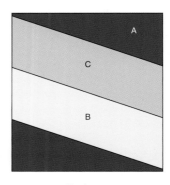

Stripes
6" x 6⅜" Finished Block
Make 24

From dark brown:
- Cut 10 (3" x 43") A strips.
- Cut 2 (1½" x 40½") F strips.
- Cut 3 (1½" x 43") G strips.
- Cut 6 (2¼" x 43") binding strips.

COMPLETING THE BLOCKS

1. Sew an A strip between a B and C strip with right sides together along the length; press seams toward A. Repeat to make 10 A-B-C strip sets.
2. Prepare template using pattern given on page 23; place the template on the strip and cut 24 A-B-C and 24 reverse A-B-C units as shown in Figure 1.

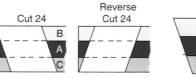

Figure 1

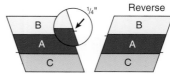

Figure 2

3. Measure and mark ¼" from the A-B seam and the A-C seam on opposite ends of A as shown in Figure 2.

4. Place a straightedge on each mark and cut from one mark to the other to make an A-B and an A-C unit as shown in Figure 3; repeat to make 24 each units and 24 each reverse units.

Figure 3

5. Join one each A-B and A-C unit to make a Stripes block as shown in Figure 4; repeat to make 24 Stripes and 24 Reverse Stripes blocks. Press seams in one direction.

Figure 4

COMPLETING THE QUILT

1. Arrange and join three Stripes blocks with three Reverse Stripes blocks to make a row as shown in Figure 5; press seams in one direction. Repeat to make eight rows.

Figure 5

2. Join the rows, turning every other row, referring to the Placement Diagram for positioning of rows; press seams in one direction. **Note:** *The A pieces will not form sharp points at the intersections of the blocks; the ends will be blunted as shown in Figure 6.*

Figure 6

3. Sew a D strip to the top and bottom of the pieced center; press seams toward D strips.

4. Join the E strips with right sides together on short ends to make one long strip; press seams open. Subcut strip into two 55½" E strips.

5. Sew the E strips to opposite long sides of the pieced center; press seams toward E strips.

6. Sew the F strips to the top and bottom of the pieced center; press seams toward F strips.

7. Join the G strips with right sides together on short ends to make one long strip; press seams open. Subcut strip into two 57½" G strips.

8. Sew the G strips to opposite long sides of the pieced center; press seams toward E strips.

9. Sew the H strips to the top and bottom of the pieced center; press seams toward H strips.

10. Join the I strips with right sides together on short ends to make one long strip; press seams open. Subcut strip into two 64" I strips.

11. Sew the I strips to opposite long sides of the pieced center to complete the pieced top; press seams toward I strips.

12. Create a quilt sandwich referring to Quilting Basics on page 46.

13. Quilt as desired.

14. Bind referring to Quilting Basics on page 46 to finish. ●

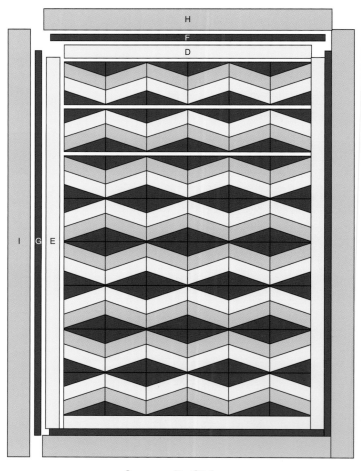

Corporal's Stripes
Assembly Diagram 48½" x 63½"

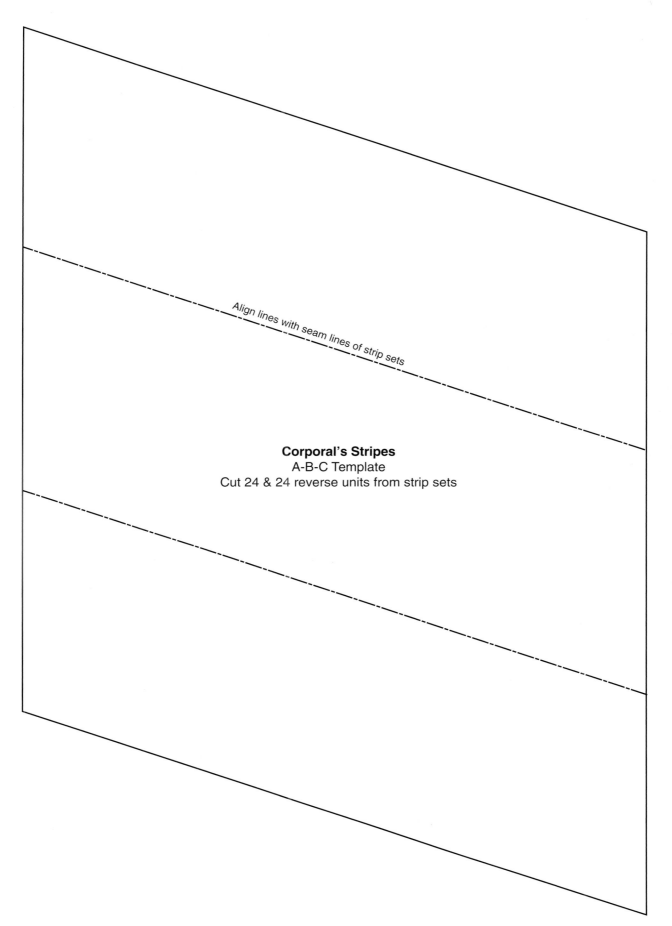

Align lines with seam lines of strip sets

Corporal's Stripes
A-B-C Template
Cut 24 & 24 reverse units from strip sets

Walk Around the Block

Showcase the rich variety of fabrics in 2½" precut strips in a gorgeous lap quilt you can whip up over a snowy weekend.

Design by Connie Kauffman

Skill Level
Beginner

Finished Size
Quilt Size: 54" x 62"
Block Size: 8" x 8" finished
Number of Blocks: 20

MATERIALS

- 27–30 (2½" x 42") medium and dark precut print and tonal strips
- ⅓ yard cream print
- ⅓ yard dark brown print
- ⅜ yard brown print
- ½ yard cream tonal
- ⅝ yard medium brown print
- ⅔ yard burgundy print
- ⅔ yard dark green print
- Backing to size
- Batting to size
- Thread
- Basic sewing tools and supplies

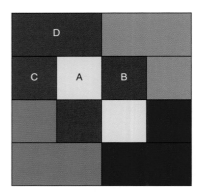

Walk Around
8" x 8" Finished Block
Make 20

CUTTING

From precut strips:
- Cut 3 each 2½" x 4½" D rectangles and 2½" C squares from each strip.
- Cut a total of 36 (2½") I squares.

From cream print:
- Cut 3 (2½" x 42") strips.
    Subcut 40 (2½") A squares.

From dark brown print:
- Cut 3 (2½" x 42") strips.
    Subcut 40 (2½") B squares.

From brown print:
- Cut 2 (2½" x 28½") G strips.
- Cut 2 (2½" x 24½") H strips.

From cream tonal:
- Cut 2 (3½" x 38½") F strips.
- Cut 2 (3½" x 40½") E strips.

From medium brown print:
- Cut 6 (2¼" x 42") L/M strips.

From dark green print:
- Cut 3 (6½" x 42") J/K strips.

COMPLETING THE BLOCKS

1. Select one each matching medium C and D pieces.
2. Sew C to B and add D to make a B-C-D unit as shown in Figure 1; press seam toward B and then D.

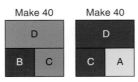

Figure 1

3. Repeat steps 1 and 2 to complete 40 B-C-D units.
4. Repeat steps 1 and 2 with dark C and D pieces and A to complete 40 A-C-D units, again referring to Figure 1.
5. To complete one Walk Around block, select two each B-C-D and A-C-D units; join one each B-C-D and A-C-D units to make a row as shown in Figure 2. Press seam toward B-C-D unit; repeat to make two rows.

Figure 2

6. Join the rows to complete one block; press seam in one direction.
7. Repeat steps 5 and 6 to complete 20 Walk Around blocks, positioning the B-C-D and A-C-D units the same in every block.

COMPLETING THE QUILT

1. Join four Walk Around blocks to make a row; press seams in one direction. Repeat to make five rows.
2. Join the rows with seams in rows going in opposite directions; press seams in one direction.
3. Sew an E strip to opposite long sides and F strips to the top and bottom of the pieced center; press seams toward E and F strips.

4. Select nine I squares; join to make an I strip. Press seams in one direction. Repeat to make four I strips.
5. Sew an I strip to one end of each G and H piece; press seams toward G and H.
6. Sew a G-I strip to opposite long sides and an H-I strip to the top and bottom of the pieced center referring to the Placement Diagram for positioning of strips; press seams toward G-I and H-I strips.
7. Join the L/M strips on short ends to make one long strip; press seams open. Subcut strip into one 50½" L strip and one 54½" M strip. Repeat with J/K strips to cut one 50½" J strip and one 54½" K strip.
8. Sew an L and J strip to opposite long sides and K and M strips to the top and bottom of the pieced center referring to the Placement Diagram to complete the pieced top; press seams toward L, J, K and M strips.
9. Create a quilt sandwich referring to Quilting Basics on page 46.
10. Quilt as desired.
11. Bind referring to Quilting Basics on page 46 to finish. ●

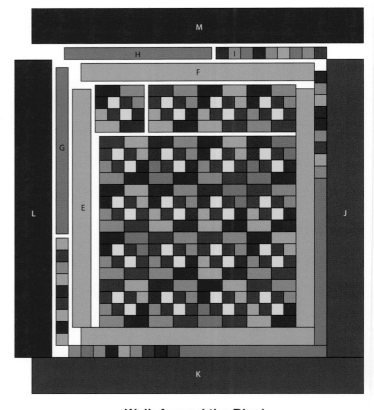

Walk Around the Block
Assembly Diagram 54" x 62"

Woven Indigo

Fresh white makes a collection of blues "pop." Take traditional colors and a simple block pattern, and create a modern quilt.

Design by Tricia Lynn Maloney

Skill Level
Beginner

Finished Size
Quilt Size: 90" x 90"
Block Size: 9" x 9" finished
Number of Blocks: 49

MATERIALS

- ¼ yard each 13 assorted medium and dark blue prints or tonals
- ¼ yard each 8 assorted blue-and-white prints
- 3⅛ yards medium blue print
- 3⅓ yards white tonal
- Backing to size
- Batting to size
- Thread
- Basic sewing tools and supplies

CUTTING

From assorted medium & dark blue prints or tonals:
- Cut 1 (3½" by fabric width) B strip from each.

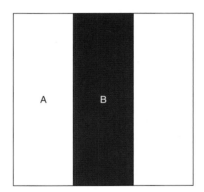

Woven Indigo
9" x 9" Finished Block
Make 49

From assorted blue-and-white prints:
- Cut 1 (3½" by fabric width) strip from each.
  Subcut strips into 12 (3½" x 16½") E rectangles,
  8 (3½" x 9½") F rectangles and 4 (3½") G squares.

From medium blue print:
- Cut 8 (9½" by fabric width) H/I strips.
- Cut 9 (2¼" by fabric width) binding strips.

From white tonal:
- Cut 26 (3½" by fabric width) A strips.
- Cut 7 (2" by fabric width) C/D strips.

COMPLETING THE BLOCKS

1. Select one B strip and two A strips. Sew an A strip to opposite long sides of B to make an A-B strip set; press seams toward B.
2. Subcut the A-B strip set into four 9½" x 9½" Woven Indigo blocks referring to Figure 1.

Figure 1

3. Repeat steps 1 and 2 to make a total of 13 A-B strip sets, and then subcut the strip sets into 49 Woven Indigo blocks.

COMPLETING THE QUILT

1. Select and join seven assorted Woven Indigo blocks to make an X row referring to Figure 2; press seams toward the upright blocks. Repeat to make a total of four X rows.
2. Repeat step 1 to complete three Y rows, again referring to Figure 2.

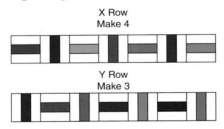

Figure 2

3. Join the X and Y rows referring to the Assembly Diagram to complete the pieced center; press seams in one direction.
4. Join the C/D strips on the short ends to make a long strip; press. Subcut strip into two 2" x 63½" C strips and two 2" x 66½" D strips.
5. Sew C strips to the top and bottom and D strips to opposite sides of the pieced center; press seams toward C and D strips.
6. Select and join three E and two F rectangles to make a side strip referring to Figure 3; press seams in one direction. Repeat to make a second side strip. Sew these strips to opposite sides of the pieced center; press seams toward the D strips.

Figure 3

7. Repeat step 6 and add a G square to each end of each strip; press seams toward G. Sew these strips to the top and bottom of the pieced center; press seams toward C strips.
8. Join the H/I strips on the short ends to make a long strip; press. Subcut strip into two each 9½" x 72½" H strips and 9½" x 90½" I strips.
9. Sew the H strips to the top and bottom, and I strips to opposite sides of the pieced center to complete the quilt top; press seams toward H and I strips.
10. Create a quilt sandwich referring to Quilting Basics on page 46.
11. Quilt as desired.
12. Bind referring to Quilting Basics on page 46 to finish. ●

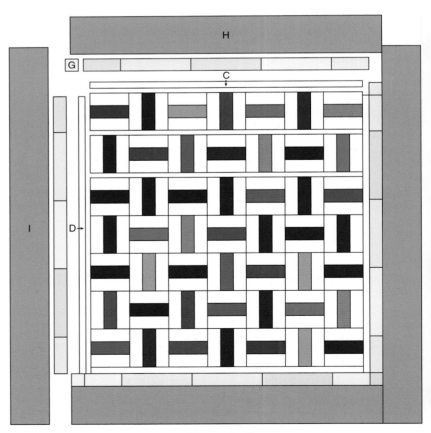

Woven Indigo
Assembly Diagram 90" x 90"

Nine-Patch Twirl

Dazzle your friends with magic. This cute quilt has what is known as a Disappearing Nine-Patch block. Can you find the Nine-Patch?

Design by Carolyn S. Vagts for The Village Pattern Company

Skill Level
Beginner

Finished Size
Quilt Size: 40½" x 53½"
Block Size: 11½" x 11½" finished
Number of Blocks: 12

MATERIALS

- 27 fat eighths (9" x 21") assorted bright colors
- ¾ yard white tonal
- Backing to size
- Batting to size
- Thread
- Basic sewing tools and supplies

CUTTING

From assorted bright colors:
- Cut 1 (4½" by fabric width) strip from each fat eighth. Subcut each strip into 4 (4½") squares to cut a total of 108 A squares.
- Cut 1 (2½" by fabric width) strip from 10 fat eighths for binding.

From white tonal:
- Cut 11 (2" by fabric width) strips. Subcut 3 strips into 8 (2" x 12") B strips. Cut 5 strips into 5 (2" x 38") C strips. Set aside 3 strips for D.

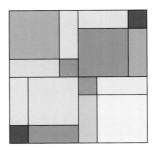

Nine-Patch Twirl
11½" x 11½" Finished Block
Make 12

COMPLETING THE BLOCKS

1. Select nine different A squares. Stitch into three rows of three A squares referring to Figure 1. Press seams in opposite directions.

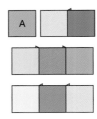

Figure 1

2. Stitch the A square rows into a Nine-Patch unit referring again to Figure 1; press seams in one direction.
3. Repeat steps 1 and 2 to make a total of 12 Nine-Patch units.

4. Rotary-cut the units in half horizontally and vertically to make four 6¼"-square quarter units per Nine-Patch unit as shown in Figure 2.

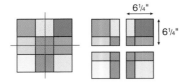

Figure 2

5. To complete one block, select four quarter units from different Nine-Patch units. Arrange the quarter units, turning them to make a Nine-Patch Twirl block referring to the block drawing and the Assembly Diagram for positioning. Stitch quarter units together as arranged to make a 12"-square block. Repeat to make 12 blocks.

COMPLETING THE QUILT

1. Stitch two B strips between three blocks to make a row as shown in Figure 3. Press seams toward B. Repeat to make a total of 4 rows.

Make 4

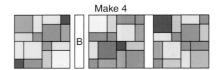

Figure 3

2. Stitch rows together with five C strips, beginning and ending with a C strip and referring to the Assembly Diagram. Press seams toward C.

3. Stitch D strips together on short ends; press seams open. Subcut strip into two 2" x 54"-long D strips.
4. Stitch a D strip on each long side of the quilt top.
5. Create a quilt sandwich referring to Quilting Basics on page 46.
6. Quilt as desired.
7. Bind referring to Quilting Basics on page 46 to finish. ●

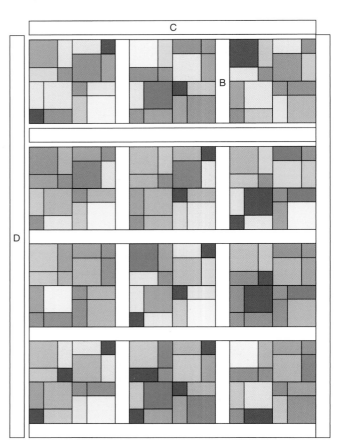

Nine-Patch Twirl
Assembly Diagram 40½" x 53½"

Chocolate Covered Cherries

One simple block in yummy fabrics makes this quilt not only delicious but quick to put together.

Design by Tricia Lynn Maloney

Skill Level
Beginner

Finished Size
Quilt Size: 54" x 72"
Block Size: 12" x 12" finished
Number of Blocks: 24

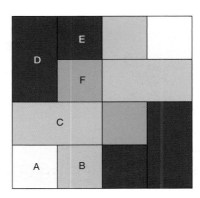

Chocolate Covered Cherries
12" x 12" Finished Block
Make 24

MATERIALS

- ½ yard light pink texture batik
- ½ yard medium pink texture batik 1
- 1⅓ yards medium pink texture batik 2
- 2⅓ yards dark brown batik
- Backing to size
- Batting to size
- Thread
- Basic sewing tools and supplies

CUTTING

From light pink texture batik:
- Cut 4 (3½" by fabric width) A strips.

From medium pink texture batik 1:
- Cut 4 (3½" by fabric width) F strips.

From medium pink texture batik 2:
- Cut 4 (3½" by fabric width) B strips.
- Cut 4 (6½" by fabric width) strips.
  Subcut strips into 48 (3½" x 6½") C rectangles.

From dark brown batik:
- Cut 4 (6½" by fabric width) strips.
  Subcut strips into 48 (3½" x 6½") D rectangles.
- Cut 8 (3½" by fabric width) strips.
  Set aside 4 strips for E.
  Set aside 4 strips for G strips.
- Cut 7 (2¼" by fabric width) binding strips.

COMPLETING THE BLOCKS

1. Sew an A strip to a B strip along length to make an A/B strip set; press seam toward B. Repeat to make a total of four A/B strip sets.

2. Repeat step 1 with E and F strips.

3. Subcut the A/B strip sets into 48 (3½" x 6½") A-B units as shown in Figure 1. Repeat with the E/F strip sets to make 48 (3½" x 6½") E-F units, again referring to Figure 1.

Figure 1

4. To complete one Chocolate Covered Cherries block, select two each C and D rectangles and A-B and E-F units.

5. Sew an A-B unit to C to make a pink unit as shown in Figure 2; press seam toward C. Repeat to make a second pink unit.

Make 2

Make 2

Figure 2   **Figure 3**

6. Sew an E-F unit to D to make a brown unit as shown in Figure 3; press seam toward D. Repeat to make a second brown unit.

7. Sew a pink unit to a brown unit to make a row as shown in Figure 4; press seam toward the brown unit. Repeat to make a second row.

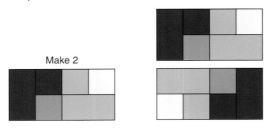

Make 2

Figure 4   **Figure 5**

8. Join the rows referring to Figure 5 to complete one Chocolate Covered Cherries block; press seam in one direction.

9. Repeat steps 4–8 to complete a total of 24 Chocolate Covered Cherries blocks.

COMPLETING THE QUILT

1. Arrange and join four Chocolate Covered Cherries blocks, turning every other block, to make a row referring to the Assembly Diagram; press seams to the right. Repeat to make a total of six rows.

2. Arrange and join the rows, turning every other row referring to the Assembly Diagram, to complete the quilt center; press seams in one direction.

3. Join G strips on the short ends to make a long strip; press. Subcut strip into two 3½" x 72½" G strips.

4. Sew a G strip to opposite long sides of the quilt center to complete the quilt top; press seams toward G strips.

5. Create a quilt sandwich referring to Quilting Basics on page 46.

6. Quilt as desired.

7. Bind referring to Quilting Basics on page 46 to finish. ●

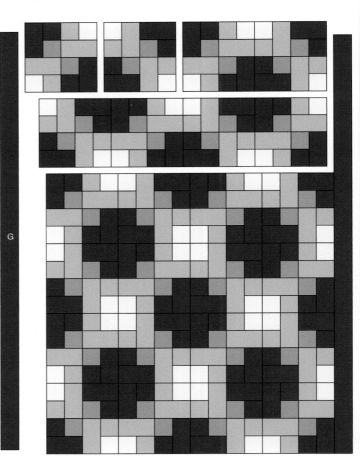

Chocolate Covered Cherries
Assembly Diagram 54" x 72"

Go Team!

This quick and easy pieced quilt made in your favorite team's colors will be a hit for any sports fan.

Designed & Quilted by Nancy Scott of Masterpiece Quilting

Skill Level
Beginner

Finished Size
Quilt Size: 40" x 65"

MATERIALS

- 1⅓ yards gold solid
- 2⅛ yards black solid
- Backing to size
- Batting to size
- Thread
- Basic sewing tools and supplies

CUTTING

From gold solid:
- Cut 2 (8½" by fabric width) strips.
  Subcut strips into 14 (5½" x 8½") C rectangles.
- Cut 1 (6½" by fabric width) strip.
  Subcut strip into 6 (5½" x 6½") D rectangles.
- Cut 2 (7½" by fabric width) strips.
  Subcut strips into 12 (5½" x 7½") E rectangles.

From black solid:
- Cut 3 (8½" by fabric width) strips.
  Subcut strips into 21 (5½" x 8½") A rectangles.
- Cut 2 (10½" by fabric width) strips.
  Subcut strips into 12 (5½" x 10½") B rectangles.
- Cut 6 (2¼" by fabric width) binding strips.

COMPLETING THE QUILT

1. Arrange and join two C rectangles and three A rectangles to make an A row referring to the Assembly Diagram; press seams toward A. Repeat to make a total of seven A rows.
2. Arrange and join one D rectangle and two each B and E rectangles to make a B row, again referring to the Assembly Diagram; press seams toward B. Repeat to make a total of six B rows.
3. Arrange and join the A and B rows, beginning and ending with A rows, to complete the quilt center; press.
4. Create a quilt sandwich referring to Quilting Basics on page 46.
5. Quilt as desired.
6. Bind referring to Quilting Basics on page 46 to finish. ●

A Row

B Row

Go Team!
Assembly Diagram 40" x 65"

Seven-Patch

This quilt is made with blocks that have only seven pieces. Twist and turn the blocks for an exceptional-looking quilt.

Design by Jen Eskridge

Skill Level
Beginner

Finished Size
Quilt Size: 75" x 90"
Block Size: 15" x 15" finished
Number of Blocks: 30

MATERIALS

- ½ yard each olive green, gray and orange solids
- 1¼ yards dark pink solid
- 5 yards white solid
- 5⅝ yards backing
- Batting 83" x 98"
- Thread
- Basic sewing tools and supplies

CUTTING

From each olive green, gray and orange solid:
- Cut 3 (3½" by fabric width) A strips.

From dark pink solid:
- Cut 3 (3½" by fabric width) A strips.
- Cut 9 (2¼" by fabric width) strips for binding.

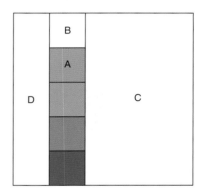

Seven-Patch
15" x 15" Finished Block
Make 30

From white solid:
- Cut 3 (3½" by fabric width) B strips.
- Cut 10 (15½" by fabric width) strips.
    Subcut 8 strips into 30 (9½" x 15½")
    C rectangles and 6 (3½" x 15½")
    D rectangles.
    Subcut 2 remaining strips into
    24 (3½" x 15½") D rectangles
    (to total 30).

COMPLETING THE BLOCKS

1. Select one A strip from each of the four colored solids and one B strip.

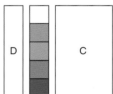

Figure 2

2. Arrange the A strips in the desired color order and sew together along length; press seams to one side. Add a B strip to one end to complete an A-B strip set. Press seam away from B. Repeat to make a total of three A-B strip sets.

3. Subcut the A-B strip sets into a total of 30 (3½" x 15½") A-B units as shown in Figure 1.

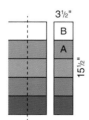

Figure 1

4. With the B square at the top, sew a D rectangle to the left edge and a C rectangle to the right edge of an A-B unit to complete one Seven-Patch block referring to Figure 2; press seams toward C and D.

5. Repeat step 4 to complete a total of 30 Seven-Patch blocks.

COMPLETING THE QUILT

1. Select and join five Seven-Patch blocks to make a row referring to the Assembly Diagram for block placement. Repeat to make six rows. Press seams in adjoining rows in opposite directions.

2. Join the rows as pieced, again referring to the Assembly Diagram to complete the quilt top; press.

3. Create a quilt sandwich referring to Quilting Basics on page 46.

4. Quilt as desired.

5. Bind referring to Quilting Basics on page 46 to finish. ●